Battles and Wars

Written by Paul Mason
Illustrated by David McAllister

**MARKS &
SPENCER**

Marks and Spencer p.l.c.
Baker Street, London W1U 8EP
www.marksandspencer.com

This book was created by Monkey Puzzle Media Ltd

ISBN 1-84273-191-2

Printed in Dubai

Designer: Sarah Crouch
Cover design: Victoria Webb
Editor: Jon Richards
Artwork commissioning:
Roger Goddard-Coote
Project manager: Alex Edmonds

Contents

Was William really a conqueror?

WILLIAM, WHO CAME FROM NORMANDY IN FRANCE, became king of England after the Battle of Hastings in 1066. Because he won, William made sure that all the stories about the battle showed him to be a great hero. He became known as William the Conqueror.

William and his men survey the newly-conquered nation.

Why didn't the English army face William straight away?

They would have, but they were busy in Yorkshire, fighting someone else. Harald Hardrada (which means 'hard ruler') had invaded from Norway after Edward the Confessor died. Harald was defeated and killed at the Battle of Stamford Bridge on September 25. Three days later William landed on the south coast.

Who wrote the Domesday Book?

William the Conqueror had the Domesday Book written when he was King of England – although William himself couldn't read. It recorded all the land and wealth in the nation.

How did William the Conqueror die?

He decided to invade France in 1087. William's horse stumbled on a hot cinder as the king led a raid in Rouen, Normandy. As the horse fell, William burst his bladder on the pommel of his saddle and he died shortly afterwards.

During William's reign he had 80 castles built across England.

Why was the battle fought at Hastings?

WILLIAM AND HIS ARMY HAD CROSSED THE ENGLISH Channel from France and landed near Hastings at Pevensey Bay. They camped there for a few weeks, built a couple of castles and waited to see if an English army would turn up to force them to return to France.

Did the Normans win the Battle of Hastings easily?

The battle only really started to go the Normans' way when the English leader, Harold, was shot in the eye with an arrow. Harold was a great leader, and without him the English didn't think they could win.

WILLIAM THE STRONG

Stories say that William the Conqueror was so strong he was able to leap on to his horse wearing a full suit of armour. Most knights had to be helped up by their servants (pages).

5

Who had the biggest army at the Battle of Agincourt?

T HE ENGLISH ARMY, UNDER THE COMMAND OF HENRY V, HAD only about 6,000 men, while the French army had 25,000 soldiers.

What was the English army doing in France?

Henry thought he had a claim to the French throne, so he invaded Normandy in August 1415. By September half his men had died in battle or of disease, and he decided to head back to England. He was on his way home when the French army caught up with him.

What happened when the two armies fought?

Amazingly, the French were massacred. They chose a terrible place for the battlefield, because it was just 1 km across. The French soldiers got so jammed in that some of them couldn't even lift their swords. The English archers fired all their arrows, then waded in with swords, hatchets and billhooks. About 1,500 French knights and 4,500 ordinary soldiers died. The English lost about 500 men.

Henry V was known as a pious man and a skilful soldier.

What's a billhook?

A tool or weapon with a curved blade that has a sharp inner edge. Sometimes they could be attached to a long pole, or they might just have a short handle. Billhooks are now generally used for pruning trees and bushes.

Why did the English boil their dead?

They didn't boil all of them, just two. The Earl of Oxford and the Duke of York were both killed. Henry didn't want to leave them in France, but he knew their bodies would rot if they were carried home. So he had them boiled until the flesh dropped off and took the skeletons home.

What happened to the prisoners?

The English took a lot of French prisoners early in the battle, and Henry had them sent to the rear of the soldiers. But then the French attacked again from in front. Henry thought the prisoners might try to attack him from behind, so he had them all killed.

Who had sent Henry a present of tennis balls?

The king of France. France and England had been at war for years (the war eventually became known as the Hundred Years' War). The message of the tennis balls was meant to be: 'Stay at home and play tennis. It will be better for you than coming to France'.

Why were England and France at war for 100 years?

The Hundred Years' War actually went on for 116 years. It started in 1337 and ended in 1453. The fighting was over who should be king of France. The kings of England thought they should rule France as well. By the time Henry V died, England controlled all of France north of the river Loire, including Paris.

TENNIS-LOVING MONARCHS

Henry was sent tennis balls by the French king as an insult. But some English monarchs actually liked playing tennis. Henry VIII was playing tennis when his wife, Anne Boleyn, was executed. The best royal tennis player was George VI, who played at Wimbledon and won a trophy.

Joan of Arc is burnt at the stake for being a witch, despite her bravery against the English during the battle at Orleans.

Who was Joan of Arc?

JOAN OF ARC WAS A BIG PROBLEM FOR THE ENGLISH. SHE LED A FRENCH army that drove them away from the city of Orleans which proved a turning point in the Hundred Years' War. From then on the English controlled less and less of France.

English warships were cramped, dark and unhygienic places to live.

How did the English defeat the Armada?

STRICTLY SPEAKING, THEY DIDN'T. THE SPANISH MADE IT TO CALAIS without losing many ships. Then the English sent fireships into the harbour and the Spanish panicked. At the Battle of Gravelines, the English sank one Spanish ship and scattered the rest. But what really did the damage was a great storm that blew the Spanish into the North Sea.

Which commander played bowls as the Spanish invaders arrived?

Legend has it that Sir Francis Drake finished a game of bowls he was playing before setting off to sea to fight the Spanish invasion fleet in 1588. Drake was one of England's greatest sea captains.

Why did the Spanish want to invade England?

King Philip of Spain wanted to invade England because it was a Protestant country, while he was a Catholic, and because England was supporting a revolt against Spanish rule in the Netherlands. The Spanish fleet – called the Armada – was on its way to Flanders. Once there, it was to have helped ferry 30,000 Spanish troops across the English Channel to invade England.

A SAILOR'S LIFE

Conditions in the English fleet were terrible. The sailors who fought against the Armada in July and August still hadn't been paid in September. Some even died of starvation because they couldn't afford to eat.

Who had the best ships, the English or the Spanish?

The Spanish had larger ships which could carry many men — up to 27,000 men were crammed into their 130 ships. The English had smaller, faster-moving ships which carried far greater numbers of cannon, and English gunners were usually very accurate.

Was the Spanish attack a surprise?

English spies had discovered the plan to invade, and the Armada was attacked before it had even left Spain. Then, when it tried to leave again, it was forced back to port by a great storm. The Spanish finally arrived in the English Channel in July 1588, just as Drake was finishing his game of bowls.

Why were the Spanish especially keen to fight Drake?

Sir Francis had spent most of the years 1585 and 1586 in the Caribbean, capturing Spanish ships and stealing their treasure. The Spanish claimed he was a pirate, but to most English people he was a hero. Queen Elizabeth I loved him too, because he kept sending her Spanish gold.

SIR WALTER RALEIGH

Raleigh was a famous Elizabethan sailor and explorer and he was a great favourite of Queen Elizabeth I. Stories say that he once laid his cloak across a puddle for the Queen so that she wouldn't get her feet wet. Unfortunately, this story isn't true. People also claim that Sir Walter brought potatoes and tobacco back to Europe from the New World. Unfortunately, this isn't true either.

How many Spanish ships made it back to Spain?

Of the 130 ships that set out, about 60 made it home. The rest had been wrecked in storms or sunk by the English. It took them so long to get home (over two months) that many of the men on board had died of starvation.

As the Spanish fled to safety, many of their ships were wrecked on rocks or sandbanks off the English coast.

Charles I is executed at Whitehall, London, in 1648.

Which king lost his head?

CHARLES I, WHO GOT INTO AN ARGUMENT WITH

Parliament and ended up being beheaded. He had summoned Parliament to help him pay for a war with Scotland, but then the parliamentarians wouldn't go away again. Eventually there was a war between the Royalists ('Cavaliers') and the Parliamentarians ('Roundheads').

CHARLES I'S NECK-BONE

The neck-bone that had been chopped through by Charles I's executioner was later used by Sir Henry Halford, as a salt shaker.

How did the Roundheads get their name?

It was from the shape of their helmets, which were round with a slight lip around the edge. They were worn by Oliver Cromwell's New Model Army.

Who was Oliver Cromwell?

Cromwell was a member of Parliament who became a successful general. He led the Roundhead forces at the Battle of Naseby in 1645, where the king's army was destroyed. Later, the king was captured, but he escaped to Scotland and tried to invade England from there. Cromwell defeated him again, at the Battle of Preston in 1648, and Charles fell into Parliament's hands once more.

Who was the 'Merry Monarch'?

What was the Rump Parliament?

The Rump Parliament was the group of Members of Parliament that was most committed to executing the king. After his death, they declared England a Commonwealth. After Cromwell and his Roundhead army had put down revolts in Scotland and Ireland, the whole of Britain became part of the Commonwealth. Cromwell was now the most powerful man in Britain.

What disease was a king's touch supposed to cure?

Scrofula, which was common when Charles II was on the throne. People used to line up to be touched by him in the hope of being cured. Unfortunately, there's no evidence that it worked. Six people were once killed when the queue they were in rushed forward and they were crushed.

Who was Lord Protector of the Commonwealth?

Oliver Cromwell, who had been a great opponent of the king's right to govern alone, became ruler in December 1653. He ruled until his death in 1658.

Why did the king wear two shirts to his execution?

He was worried he'd shiver in the cold January air and the crowds that had gathered to watch the execution would think he was scared. Charles had written his last words on a sheet of paper so that he wouldn't forget them. But in the end he said them in a whisper and no one heard.

Who decided to execute the king?

Parliament, but only just. In fact, the decision to execute Charles was made by just one vote.

CHARLES II, WHO BECAME KING TWO YEARS AFTER CROMWELL'S DEATH.
He was the son of Charles I, and had fought for him during the Civil War when the Roundheads fought the Cavaliers. He was said to have escaped capture by the Roundheads on one occasion by spending days hiding up a tree.

Charles II, the first king after the Royalists regained power, hides from Cromwell's army up a tree.

Paul Revere rides to warn the Minutemen that the British forces are approaching.

Which tea party started a war?

THE AMERICAN WAR OF INDEPENDENCE, ALSO CALLED THE AMERICAN

Revolution, began in 1775. America was an British colony at the time. To protest about the amount of taxes they had to pay to the British government, a group of Americans dressed up as Native Americans and dumped a load of tea into Boston Harbour in 1773. This became known as the Boston Tea Party.

THE MAD KING?

❖

George III, who was king of Britain during the American War of Independence, went through periods when he seemed mad. He once told his courtiers that he was going to adopt a new son, named Octavius. They were surprised to discover that Octavius was, in fact, a pillow.

Who was Paul Revere?

One of the people who had dressed up as a Native American for the Boston Tea Party. He later became famous for riding to warn the Minutemen (American patriots) of the approach of British forces. His warning meant that the Minutemen were ready the next morning to fight a battle at Lexington Green. This battle started the War of Independence.

Why did the Americans dress up as Native Americans?

It was meant to be a disguise. The protesters didn't want to be put in prison or executed, so they pretended to be Native Americans. They thought no one would notice that they were actually white men.

Who were the Minutemen?

A group of Americans who were trained to be ready at a minute's warning to fight the British. They were guerillas who knew the country far better than the British troops. The British found them very difficult to fight, because the Minutemen didn't behave like an ordinary army. They usually appeared, shot a few soldiers, then disappeared again.

What did General Cornwallis get for Christmas?

A nasty surprise. Cornwallis was an British general who had driven the American rebel forces back across the river Delaware by December 1776. On Christmas night, the American General Washington recrossed the Delaware and attacked Cornwallis. He took 1,000 British soldiers prisoner.

Who were 'George's friends'?

A group of people in England who were close to King George III. They advised him to take a harsh line with the American rebels, instead of trying to reach an agreement with them. In the end, the advice of George's friends lost him all his territories south of the Canadian border.

Who helped the Americans?

A German soldier named Baron Friedrich von Steuben gave American troops important training in the winter of 1777–1778. But the most important foreign helpers were the French, who supported the revolution all along, and actually declared war on England in June 1778.

Who became king of America?

N O ONE. THE AMERICANS DIDN'T WANT A KING, EVEN THOUGH almost everyone else had one. Instead, they voted for a president. The first one was George Washington, who had been one of their best generals. They decided to vote for the president every four years.

George Washington – a brilliant military commander. He was elected first US president in April 1789.

13

THE VICTORY

Admiral Lord Nelson's warship, HMS *Victory*, was launched in 1765, making her 40 years old at the Battle of Trafalgar. After bringing Admiral Nelson's body home, she sailed back to carry on the fight against Napoleon Bonaparte. The *Victory* is now in dry dock in Portsmouth, England.

Who is said to have asked to be kissed on his deathbed?

Admiral Lord Nelson, the hero of the English Navy. He had just been shot and realised he was about to die. Legend has it that he said 'Kiss me, Hardy'. Hardy was one of his officers, and was holding Nelson in his arms. Actually, Nelson's last words were 'Thank God I have done my duty.'

What was a cat o' nine tails?

A special whip with nine separate strands of leather. It was used to punish sailors who had broken the ship's rules. After he had been flogged, salt was rubbed into a man's back to stop the wound from getting infected.

Which admiral couldn't see a signal visible to everyone else?

An old injury made Nelson blind in one eye. At the Battle of Copenhagen in 1801, Nelson's commanding officer ordered him to withdraw, thinking the battle was lost. Nelson placed his telescope to his blind eye and claimed not to be able to see the signal, then carried on to win the battle.

How did Nelson come to be shot at Trafalgar?

NELSON WAS LEADING THE BRITISH NAVY AGAINST A LARGER FRENCH FLEET AT Trafalgar, in 1805. The British fleet had been sent to attack the French and protect England from the invasion which Napoleon was said to be planning. Nelson divided his fleet in two and they attacked the French fleet. Nelson's ship, HMS *Victory*, was in a skirmish with two French warships and he was shot by a sniper during a battle with the French ship *Redoutable*.

What was life like in the British Navy?

Life was very tough for ordinary sailors. The work was hard, the food was terrible and there wasn't enough space. Only the captain had his own cabin, and on most ships even that wasn't much bigger than a cupboard. Discipline was strict and anyone who broke the ship's rules was severely punished. Men could be flogged (whipped) with a cat o' nine tails, or even hanged.

What happened when Nelson died?

THE NATION WENT INTO MOURNING. HE was England's greatest naval commander, and had twice stopped Napoleon Bonaparte from invading Britain. To honour his memory, a huge column was erected in London. The column is called Nelson's Column and it still stands in Trafalgar Square today.

Who won the Battle of Trafalgar?

Nelson had 27 ships and the French had 33. He split his force in two and attacked both ends of the French line of ships. When the battle was at its most fierce, Nelson raised a famous signal: 'England expects that every man will do his duty'. The French were cut to pieces in the fighting that followed. They lost 20 ships and about 14,000 men. The British lost about 1,500 men, including Nelson, but no ships.

s battle it out at Trafalgar while
son lies dying.

Did many people want to join the Navy?

Plenty of young men wanted to be officers, but very few ordinary sailors wanted to join the Navy. Many were forced to join by 'press gangs', which were sent ashore to kidnap men who were then forced to work on the ships.

Napoleon, brooding on the island of Elba, plans for his return to power.

Which French leader returned to fight another day?

NAPOLEON BONAPARTE, WHO HAD BEEN

ruler of France (and most of Europe) from 1804 to 1814. He was finally defeated in April 1814 and exiled to the Mediterranean island of Elba. But Napoleon escaped and returned to France in 1815.

How did the French react to Napoleon's return?

Many people were delighted, and lots of Napoleon's old soldiers rejoined his army. In the rest of Europe they weren't so pleased. Austria, Britain, Prussia and Russia decided to send an army to defeat the French. Napoleon's spies told him of the plan and he led an army to attack the allied force. The armies met at a place called Waterloo.

What was the Old Guard?

Napoleon's best troops and his personal bodyguards. They were kept in reserve to be used only when they were most badly needed.

Were many people killed at the Battle of Waterloo?

The fighting lasted from June 15 to 18. It was one of the bloodiest battles in history. On the last day alone, 40,000 French soldiers and 22,000 allied soldiers were killed. At one point about 45,000 men were lying dead or wounded within an area of 8 square kilometres.

GEORGE IV AND THE BIG LIE

❖

King George IV was a terrible liar. Even though he was so fat he could barely sit on a horse, he used to tell people that he had led a cavalry charge at the Battle of Waterloo. 'Isn't that true, Wellington?' he asked one of his star generals. The duke's clever reply was: 'I have often heard you say so, your majesty.'

Who won the Battle of Waterloo?

The allies, although for much of the fighting it was impossible to tell who was likely to win. Mistakes by two of Napoleon's commanders and Wellington's clever tactics meant that in the end Napoleon was being attacked from so many sides he was defeated. He only escaped thanks to the bravery of the Old Guard.

Was Napoleon banished to Elba again?

No, he was captured by the allies and sent to live on the island of St Helena, right in the middle of the Atlantic Ocean. It was so far away that it would be impossible for him to return to France in secret and start yet another war.

Who led the allied army at Waterloo?

GENERAL ARTHUR WELLESLEY, THE DUKE OF WELLINGTON. HE HAD already successfully defeated Napoleon's forces during the Peninsula War where Wellington's armies had forced the French out of Spain.

Wellington and his commanders survey the battlefield at Waterloo.

Which Nightingale worked at the Battle of Balaklava?

Florence Nightingale tends wounded soldiers at Scutari hospital during the Crimean War.

THE NURSE FLORENCE NIGHTINGALE

brought aid to the wounded after the battle, which was during the Crimean War in 1854, in what is now Russia. She had heard reports of the terrible conditions the soldiers endured and volunteered to take 38 nurses with her to help those injured in battle.

What happened to Florence Nightingale after the war?

She returned to England in 1860, as the war finished. The public donated money with which she started Britain's first school for nurses, at St Thomas' Hospital in London.

Which General wasn't sure who he was fighting?

Lord Raglan, the British commander, was 67 years old and a bit senile. Raglan had fought against France during the Napoleonic wars 40 years earlier, and he insisted on calling the enemy 'the French', even though the French were actually on his side.

What was the Charge of the Light Brigade?

THE LIGHT BRIGADE WAS A UNIT OF CAVALRY IN THE BRITISH ARMY.

They were ordered to charge along a valley to attack a Russian position, but almost all were killed by the Russian guns. The poet Alfred Tennyson wrote a famous poem about what heroes the men of the Light Brigade were.

What was it like being a soldier in the Crimean War?

Life was terrible for the ordinary soldiers. They rarely had enough to eat, and during the winter they shivered in the cold air. In summertime, many soldiers died of dysentery, because there were very few proper toilets and the water supplies became contaminated. More soldiers died of sickness than of battle injuries.

Did the soldiers protest about the conditions?

Not if they had any sense. The British Army still allowed soldiers to be flogged (whipped) if their commanding officer thought it right. All other European countries had stopped this by the time the British finally gave it up in 1881.

Soldiers line up in readiness for the Charge of the Light Brigade.

THE CHARGE OF THE LIGHT BRIGADE – STUPID OR BRAVE?

The Charge of the Light Brigade became a famous poem by Alfred Tennyson, which asked 'When can their glory fade? Oh, the wild charge they made!' A French general named Bosquet, who watched the charge, had a slightly different view: 'It's magnificent, but it isn't war – it's stupidity.'

How did people at home find out about the war?

Through journalists. The Crimean War was the first war in which journalists accompanied the soldiers and witnessed the fighting. They sent back reports of the terrible conditions that shocked people at home and led to pressure on the government to end the war quickly.

Zulu warriors were famed for their bravery and ferocity.

Who cleaned their spears on the tunics of English soldiers?

THE ZULU WARRIORS OF CETSHWAYO, IN 1879. THE ZULUS WON A HUGE battle against the British Army, at a place called Ishandlwana. They called this great battle 'The Washing Of The Spears', because so much blood was shed.

Who was Shaka Zulu?

The great warrior-leader of the Zulu people, who died in 1828. He had built the Zulu empire up from a small territory to a huge nation with a large, efficient army. By the time Cetshwayo became leader, the Zulus controlled over 50,000 square kilometres of southern Africa, and their empire was growing.

What was the Battle of Rorke's Drift?

One hundred and thirty-nine soldiers defended the base against an army of 4,000 warriors. Eleven Victoria Crosses were awarded to soldiers who fought at Rorke's Drift. The Victoria Cross is the highest honour a British soldier can get.

MFECANE – 'THE CRUSHING'

During the early 1800s the Zulu empire was expanding. The British had established bases at Durban and Cape Town, and the Dutch had trekked north in covered wagons searching for farmland. Several peoples were squeezed out by the newcomers, and found new homes as far away as Zimbabwe, Mozambique and Zambia. The Zulus called this process *mfecane* – which means 'the crushing'.

Why were the British fighting the Zulus?

T HEY WANTED THE SAME LAND AS THE ZULUS. SOUTHERN AFRICA HAD rich farmland and, even better, gold and diamonds had been discovered there. To get control of the area the British sent 5,000 European and 10,000 African soldiers into Zulu territory.

How did Zulus armed with spears beat soldiers with rifles and machine guns?

The Zulus sprung a neat trap on the British. About 2,000 British troops were camped at a place called Ishandlwana. They spotted a small group of Zulus in the distance and some men were sent after them. As the pursuers chased the Zulus over a crest, they stopped dead in their tracks. Below them was crouched an army of 20,000 Zulu warriors.

How many soldiers died at Ishandlwana?

About 1,400 men were massacred. The rest fled – some were killed later by the Zulus, others found their way to a place called Rorke's Drift. This was a British base on the Buffalo river.

What was an *assegai*?

A Zulu spear, which was used together with a long shield for hand-to-hand fighting. It had a long, broad blade and a fairly short handle, and could be used for stabbing or throwing.

A British soldier with a bayonet faces a Zulu warrior with a spear.

The Mahdi or 'divinely guided one' intended to banish the Anglo-Egyptian forces from the Sudan.

What earned Gordon the name Chinese Gordon?

He had fought in the 'Arrow War' in China, and was there when the British occupied Peking (now called Beijing). Gordon got the job of burning down the Chinese emperor's summer palace, as a way of teaching him a lesson for defying the British.

What was the Ever-Victorious Army?

A group of Chinese peasants led by Gordon, who defended the European trading city of Shanghai against attack during the Taiping Rebellion. Gordon led the Ever-Victorious Army for 18 months, until the rebellion had been crushed. It was never defeated and he returned to England a hero.

Why was a British general made governor of the Sudan?

Because the ruler of Egypt, who was called the Khedive, was kept in power by the British. He often employed British officers, and when he needed a new governor of Sudan, Gordon got the job. Gordon was already a hero in Britain following his bravery in the Crimean War and China.

What was the Siege of Khartoum?

When he arrived in Khartoum, the capital of Sudan, Gordon's aim was to evacuate the city before the Mahdi arrived. He knew he couldn't win a battle with his much smaller forces. Two thousand women, children and sick people were evacuated, but then the Mahdi's army arrived in March 1884. They put Khartoum under siege, and it stayed under siege for almost a year.

Who made the Mahdi mad?

THE BRITISH GENERAL CHARLES GORDON, WHO WAS ALSO KNOWN AS Chinese Gordon. The Mahdi was the leader of a group of Sudanese fighters who wanted to take control of their country away from the Egyptians. Gordon had been appointed governor-general of Sudan by the Egyptian ruler.

Did the British send an army to help Gordon?

Not at first. The prime minister, William Gladstone, had only reluctantly agreed to let Gordon go to Sudan, and he didn't want to send anyone to help. But by August, Gladstone was forced to act on pressure from the public and Queen Victoria.

Was Khartoum saved?

No. The relief army arrived too late. The Mahdi had been about to call off the siege when the level of the Nile, which flowed past the city, dropped. A gap in the battlements opened, and the Mahdi's forces made one last attack and broke into the city. The relief army arrived two days later.

What happened to the people of Khartoum?

Most of them were massacred. The Mahdi had been going to have Khartoum as his capital, but the smell of dead bodies was so bad that he had to move to the nearby city of Omdurman.

GLADSTONE

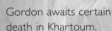

The slow speed with which William Gladstone sent help to Gordon cost him dear. It was so unpopular with the British public that it was part of the reason for him losing the next election!

What happened to Chinese Gordon?

THE MAHDI HAD EXPRESSLY SAID THAT HE DID NOT WANT GORDON TO BE killed if Khartoum was captured. Unfortunately, the attackers didn't take any notice of this command. Gordon was slaughtered with the rest of the city's defenders.

Gordon awaits certain death in Khartoum.

Life in the trenches was horrific for the soldiers. They suffered from cold, lack of clean water, disease and hunger.

Which 'lions' were led by 'donkeys'?

B RITISH SOLDIERS DURING THE FIRST WORLD WAR (1914–1918).

Although the soldiers were famously brave, their generals were also famously stupid. A German officer once compared the British Army with lions (the soldiers) being led by donkeys (the generals).

Why were the British generals stupid?

They had expected the war to be over quickly, but when the armies met, neither could get the upper hand. Instead, they dug in along what became known as the Western Front.

What was a war of attrition?

The idea was that if you had a battle where you lost 10,000 men and the enemy lost 12,000 men, you had won the battle even if no one had gained any territory. Eventually, the enemy would run out of soldiers, and the war would be over. The generals stuck with this idea for several years.

What was the worst battle?

For the British, the bloodiest battle was the Somme (July–September 1916). The greatest number of British soldiers ever killed in a battle died there. 20,000 soldiers died and 60,000 were injured on the first day alone.

How many shells were fired at the Battle of the Somme?

During the 'softening-up' attack on the German trenches, 1,700,000 shells were fired over a period of eight days. No one is sure exactly how many shells were fired during the whole battle.

What new weapon did the British use?

Tanks were used for the first time at the Somme. They weren't very successful – half of them failed even to start, and others broke down in no-man's land (the land between the two sides). But people began to see how they could be very useful in a battle.

OVER THE TOP

The soldiers called the moment when they had to climb out of their trenches and attack 'going over the top'. It was so dangerous that they often wrote farewell letters to their families before an attack. One soldier wrote to his wife: 'We are going over the top this afternoon and only God in Heaven knows who will come out alive'.

Was the Somme the worst battle of the war?

Possibly Not. At the Battle of Passchendaele (July–Nov 1917) over 24,000 men died on the first day. The poet Siegfried Sassoon wrote: 'I died in hell – they called it Passchendaele'. For the French army, the Battle of Verdun (Feb–Dec 1916) was the worst – over 500,000 men died.

What was no-man's land?

The space between the opposing trenches. Often it was quite narrow and, at Christmas, the soldiers could hear the other side singing carols. No man's land was filled with bomb craters, barbed wire, mines and dead bodies.

How many men died at the Somme?

In total, over 1,000,000 men were killed. When it was over, the Allies had won a strip of land approximately 35 kilometres long and 19 kilometres wide. Over 3,000 men died for each square kilometre.

British troops attacking a German trench.

THE BLITZ

The Blitz – a series of heavy bombing raids on London – began on September 7, 1940. The Luftwaffe thought that it could force Fighter Command to defend London in large numbers, which would give the opportunity to shoot down more British fighters. The RAF had also bombed Berlin, which made Hitler so furious that he decided to switch his attacks to London.

What was a 'scramble'?

WHEN FIGHTER COMMAND GOT WARNING OF APPROACHING German planes they telephoned through to the airfield. When the phone rang and the order 'Scramble!' was given, the pilots dropped everything and climbed into their planes.

Who kept score during the Battle of Britain?

Every day the newspapers carried headlines like 'Luftwaffe 10, RAF 124'. The numbers of German planes shot down were rarely as high as claimed, but during two of the heaviest days of fighting – August 15 and 16, 1940 – two Luftwaffe planes were shot down for every RAF plane. By late August, the Luftwaffe had lost over 600 aircraft while the RAF had lost just 260.

Which pilots stopped a Sealion invading Britain?

The pilots of Fighter Command, part of the Royal Air Force (RAF). The Germans wanted to invade Britain during the Second World War – the invasion was codenamed Operation Sealion. But they needed control of the skies, which meant that they had to beat the RAF.

RAF pilots get ready to take off whilst under fire from German bombers.

26

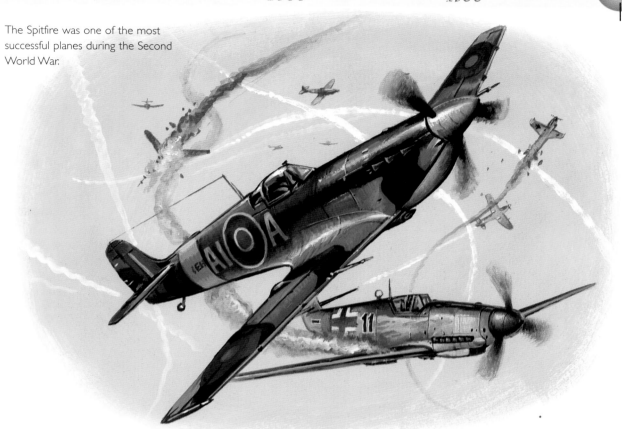

The Spitfire was one of the most successful planes during the Second World War.

What kind of planes took part in the Battle of Britain?
On the British side, Hurricanes and Spitfires. The Germans had Messerschmidt fighters and Heinkel bombers. The Spitfire was the plane the Luftwaffe pilots feared most: it was fast and manoeuvrable.

What nationality were the RAF pilots?
Most were British, but there were pilots from elsewhere too. There were Poles and Czechs, among others, who had escaped when their countries were overrun by the Germans.

Were the British well prepared for the Battle of Britain?
In June 1940, a month before the Battle of Britain began, the chief of Fighter Command told the government that if the Germans attacked he wouldn't be able to keep air superiority for more than 24 hours. But by the time the battle started, 715 planes were available, with 424 ready to be built.

What was the Battle of Britain?

FROM JULY TO SEPTEMBER 1940 THE LUFTWAFFE (GERMAN AIR FORCE) tried to get control of the skies over the English Channel and southern England. The air battles between the RAF and the Luftwaffe became known as the Battle of Britain.

Why did the Germans stop using Stukas?
The Germans did use their Stuka dive-bomber planes at first, but on August 18th 1940, 87 Stukas were shot down. The Germans only used them again on very rare occasions.

THE FINAL DAY

The Battle of Britain effectively ended on September 15, 1940. In a day of heavy fighting Fighter Command shot down over 60 Luftwaffe planes. The Germans realised that they would not be able to control the skies over the Channel, and shelved their plans to invade Britain.

General Bernard Montgomery

General Erwin Rommel

Who was Monty?

MONTY WAS THE NICKNAME OF THE BRITISH COMMANDER OF THE 8th Army in Africa, General Bernard Montgomery. After leading the defeat of Rommel at the Battle of El Alamein, he went on to command the British and Canadian forces on D-Day.

Who were the Desert Rats?

The Desert Rats was the nickname of the 7th Armoured Division of the British Army. They were first called rats by the Nazi radio broadcaster Lord Haw-Haw, as an insult. But they liked the name so much that they decided to keep it.

Who was the Desert Fox?

The German general, Erwin Rommel. He was called the Desert Fox by both the British and the Germans, because of his cunning surprise attacks. He was so successful that Hitler quickly promoted him to Field Marshal.

What was the Battle of El Alamein?

Rommel was ordered by Hitler to attack the British in Cairo, their main base in North Africa. He was stopped within 100 kilometres of the city, at a place called El Alamein, in 1942. Although the British were pleased, many Arabs were disappointed: they saw Rommel as a liberator who would free them from the British.

How did Rommel almost become the ruler of Germany?

In 1944 some of Rommel's friends suggested that if Hitler were overthrown he should become German leader. Unknown to Rommel, these same friends were plotting to assassinate Hitler. But Hitler survived, and Rommel was arrested. He took poison in prison and died, to save his family from punishment.

What was the Battle of Tobruk?

Tobruk was the last city in north Africa unconquered by the Africa Korps, Rommel's army. It was guarded by the 9th Australian Division. If Tobruk had been captured, the Germans might have been able to attack the British in Egypt.

LORD HAW-HAW

Lord Haw-Haw was an Englishman who supported Hitler and went to live in Germany. He sent radio broadcasts to Britain saying that Germany was about to win the war and that Britain should surrender. His real name was William Joyce, but his 'posh' accent was so ridiculous that people called him Lord Haw-Haw.

How did Hitler survive being assassinated?

By sheer luck he was shielded from the force of the bomb that went off in his command centre.

Towards the end of the battle at El Alamein, the Germans had only 90 tanks against the Allied forces' 800.

The *Graf Spee* explodes having been scuttled by her commander.

Why did a German commander sink his own ship?

He thought (wrongly) that there was a powerful British fleet waiting for him just over the horizon. Hitler ordered him not to surrender because the ship would then be captured by the British. The only other option was to sink the ship.

What's a pocket battleship?

After losing the First World War Germany was forbidden to build full-sized battleships. Instead, they built pocket battleships – smaller, well-armed versions.

Who served up their battleship on a plate?

THE GERMAN NAVY. THE POCKET BATTLESHIP *GRAF SPEE* WAS scuttled (deliberately sunk) by her commander near the mouth of the River Plate in Uruguay, in December 1939.

How did the Royal Navy find the Graf Spee?

A merchant ship managed to send out a signal 'R-R-R', indicating an attack by a raider, before she was sunk. Three ships, HMS *Exeter*, HMS *Ajax* and HMNZS *Achilles*, set off in pursuit. After the Battle of the River Plate, the three ships managed to chase the *Graf Spee* into Montevideo harbour.

SNORKELLING SUBMARINES!

Near to the end of the war, German U-boats were fitted with a device called a snorkel. This allowed them to stay below the surface for long periods, but it came too late to save Germany from defeat.

How successful was the *Bismarck*?

In her first battle, the *Bismarck* sank HMS *Hood*, a British battle cruiser sent to intercept it. But the Royal Navy was closing in on the *Bismarck* – almost the entire Home Fleet had set off in pursuit. The *Bismarck*'s steering gear was wrecked by torpedo planes, and she could only turn in a large circle. Within a few hours the British had caught up.

How many U-boats did the Royal Navy destroy?

Germany built 1,162 U-boats, of which 785 were destroyed or captured. Of these 41 were destroyed in the month of May 1943 alone. After this, the wolf packs were never such a dangerous threat to Allied shipping.

Which was the most powerful German battleship ever?

The *Bismarck*, which joined the German Navy in August 1940. She had eight 15-inch guns and twelve 5.9-inch guns, as well as numerous other weapons.

How was the *Bismarck* sunk?

With a combination of torpedoes and gunfire from British battleships. The *Bismarck*'s crew realised their ship was a flaming wreck and set off explosions inside the hull. Within a short time the *Bismarck* had sunk.

What were the wolf packs?

GROUPS OF GERMAN SUBMARINES (CALLED U-BOATS) WHICH

attacked Allied ships during the Battle of the Atlantic. They waited in a line across the shipping lanes until one of the U-boats spotted a convoy of ships. A radio message called the other subs, and when enough had gathered, they launched an attack on the convoy.

A U-boat comes to the surface having torpedoed an Allied ship.

Index